This Wedding Planner Belongs To:

_____

Initial Planning Phase

IDEAS FOR THEME

IDEAS FOR VENUE

IDEAS FOR COLORS

IDEAS FOR MUSIC

IDEAS FOR RECEPTION

OTHER IDEAS

Notes & Ideas

Wedding Budget Planner
Expense MANAGER

CATEGORY/ITEMS	BUDGET	ACTUAL COST	BALANCE

Wedding Budget Checklist

CATEGORY	BUDGET	ACTUAL COST	DEPOSIT	BALANCE

Wedding Contact List

IMPORTANT VENDOR CONTACTS				
	NAME	PHONE #	EMAIL	ADDRESS
OFFICIANT				
RECEPTION VENUE				
BRIDAL SHOP				
SEAMSTRESS				
FLORIST				
CATERER				
DJ/ENTERTAINMENT				
WEDDING VENUE				
TRANSPORTATION				
OTHER:				
OTHER:				
OTHER:				

NOTES & More

SPECIAL REMINDERS

Planning Snapshot

CEREMONY EXPENSE TRACKER					
	BUDGET	COST	DEPOSIT	BALANCE	DUE DATE
OFFICIANT GRATUITY					
MARRIAGE LICENSE					
VENUE COST					
FLOWERS					
DECORATIONS					
OTHER					

NOTES & Reminders

NOTES & REMINDERS

RECEPTION EXPENSE TRACKER					
	BUDGET	COST	DEPOSIT	BALANCE	DUE DATE
VENUE FEE					
CATERING/FOOD					
BAR/BEVERAGES					
CAKE/CUTTING FEE					
DECORATIONS					
RENTALS/EXTRAS					
BARTENDER/STAFF					

NOTES & More

SPECIAL REMINDERS

Planning Snapshot

PAPER PRODUCTS EXPENSE TRACKER

	BUDGET	COST	DEPOSIT	BALANCE	DUE DATE
INVITATIONS/CARDS					
POSTAGE COSTS					
THANK YOU CARDS					
PLACE CARDS					
GUESTBOOK					
OTHER					

NOTES & Reminders

NOTES & REMINDERS

ENTERTAINMENT EXPENSE TRACKER

	BUDGET	COST	DEPOSIT	BALANCE	DUE DATE
BAND/DJ					
SOUND SYSTEM RENTAL					
VENUE/DANCE RENTAL					
GRATUITIES					
OTHER:					
OTHER:					
OTHER:					

NOTES & More

SPECIAL REMINDERS

Planning Snapshot

WEDDING PARTY ATTIRE EXPENSE TRACKER

	BUDGET	COST	DEPOSIT	BALANCE	DUE DATE
WEDDING DRESS					
TUX RENTALS					
BRIDESMAID DRESSES					
SHOES/HEELS					
VEIL/GARTER/OTHER					
ALTERATION COSTS					

NOTES *& Reminders*

NOTES & REMINDERS

TRANSPORTATION EXPENSE TRACKER

	BUDGET	COST	DEPOSIT	BALANCE	DUE DATE
LIMO RENTAL					
VALET PARKING					
VENUE TRANSPORTATION					
AIRPORT TRANSPORTATION					
OTHER:					
OTHER:					
OTHER:					

NOTES *& More*

SPECIAL REMINDERS

Planning Snapshot

FLORIST EXPENSE TRACKER

	BUDGET	COST	DEPOSIT	BALANCE	DUE DATE
BOUQUETS					
VENUE DECORATIONS					
BOUTONNIERES					
VASES/EXTRAS					
TABLE DECORATIONS					
OTHER:					

NOTES & Reminders

NOTES & REMINDERS

OTHER EXPENSE TRACKER

	BUDGET	COST	DEPOSIT	BALANCE	DUE DATE
PHOTOGRAPHER					
VIDEOGRAPHER					
CATERER					
HAIR/MAKEUP/SALON					
WEDDING RINGS					
WEDDING PARTY GIFTS					
OTHER:					

NOTES & More

SPECIAL REMINDERS

Bride's Planner

HAIR APPOINTMENT

SALON NAME	DATE	TIME	BOOKED FOR:	ADDRESS:
			☐	
			☐	
			☐	

NOTES

MAKE UP APPOINTMENT

SALON NAME	DATE	TIME	BOOKED FOR:	ADDRESS:
			☐	
			☐	
			☐	

NOTES

MANICURE/PEDICURE APPOINTMENT

SALON NAME	DATE	TIME	BOOKED FOR:	ADDRESS:
			☐	
			☐	
			☐	

NOTES

Groom's Planner

HAIR APPOINTMENT

SALON NAME	DATE	TIME	BOOKED FOR:	ADDRESS:
			☐	
			☐	
			☐	

NOTES

TUX FITTING APPOINTMENT

BUSINESS NAME	DATE	TIME	BOOKED FOR:	ADDRESS:
			☐	
			☐	

NOTES

OTHER:

BUSINESS NAME	DATE	TIME	BOOKED FOR:	ADDRESS:
			☐	
			☐	
			☐	

NOTES

Important Dates

DATE:	DATE:	DATE:	REMINDERS
DATE:	DATE:	DATE:	
DATE:	DATE:	DATE:	
			NOTES
DATE:	DATE:	DATE:	
DATE:	DATE:	DATE:	

Weekly Wedding Planning

WEEK OF: _____

MONDAY

TUESDAY

WEDNESDAY

THURSDAY

FRIDAY

SATURDAY

WEDDING TO DO LIST

☐ _____
☐ _____
☐ _____
☐ _____
☐ _____
☐ _____
☐ _____
☐ _____
☐ _____
☐ _____
☐ _____
☐ _____
☐ _____
☐ _____
☐ _____
☐ _____
☐ _____

APPOINTMENTS & MEETINGS

DATE	TIME	VENDOR	PURPOSE

Weekly Wedding Planning

WEEK OF: _____

MONDAY

TUESDAY

WEDNESDAY

THURSDAY

FRIDAY

SATURDAY

WEDDING TO DO LIST

- [ ] _____
- [ ] _____
- [ ] _____
- [ ] _____
- [ ] _____
- [ ] _____
- [ ] _____
- [ ] _____
- [ ] _____
- [ ] _____
- [ ] _____
- [ ] _____
- [ ] _____
- [ ] _____
- [ ] _____
- [ ] _____

APPOINTMENTS & MEETINGS

DATE	TIME	VENDOR	PURPOSE

Weekly Wedding Planning

WEEK OF: _____

MONDAY

TUESDAY

WEDNESDAY

THURSDAY

FRIDAY

SATURDAY

WEDDING TO DO LIST

- [ ]
- [ ]
- [ ]
- [ ]
- [ ]
- [ ]
- [ ]
- [ ]
- [ ]
- [ ]
- [ ]
- [ ]
- [ ]
- [ ]
- [ ]
- [ ]
- [ ]
- [ ]

APPOINTMENTS & MEETINGS

DATE	TIME	VENDOR	PURPOSE

Weekly Wedding Planning

WEEK OF: _____

MONDAY

TUESDAY

WEDNESDAY

THURSDAY

FRIDAY

SATURDAY

WEDDING TO DO LIST

- [ ] _____
- [ ] _____
- [ ] _____
- [ ] _____
- [ ] _____
- [ ] _____
- [ ] _____
- [ ] _____
- [ ] _____
- [ ] _____
- [ ] _____
- [ ] _____
- [ ] _____
- [ ] _____
- [ ] _____
- [ ] _____
- [ ] _____
- [ ] _____

APPOINTMENTS & MEETINGS

DATE	TIME	VENDOR	PURPOSE

Weekly Wedding Planning

WEEK OF: _____

MONDAY

TUESDAY

WEDNESDAY

THURSDAY

FRIDAY

SATURDAY

WEDDING TO DO LIST

☐ _____
☐ _____
☐ _____
☐ _____
☐ _____
☐ _____
☐ _____
☐ _____
☐ _____
☐ _____
☐ _____
☐ _____
☐ _____
☐ _____
☐ _____
☐ _____
☐ _____
☐ _____

APPOINTMENTS & MEETINGS

DATE	TIME	VENDOR	PURPOSE

Weekly Wedding Planning

WEEK OF: _____

MONDAY

WEDDING TO DO LIST

- [ ] _____
- [ ] _____
- [ ] _____
- [ ] _____
- [ ] _____
- [ ] _____
- [ ] _____
- [ ] _____
- [ ] _____
- [ ] _____
- [ ] _____
- [ ] _____
- [ ] _____
- [ ] _____
- [ ] _____
- [ ] _____
- [ ] _____

TUESDAY

WEDNESDAY

THURSDAY

APPOINTMENTS & MEETINGS			
DATE	TIME	VENDOR	PURPOSE

FRIDAY

SATURDAY

Weekly Wedding Planning

WEEK OF: _____

MONDAY

TUESDAY

WEDNESDAY

THURSDAY

FRIDAY

SATURDAY

WEDDING TO DO LIST

- [ ]
- [ ]
- [ ]
- [ ]
- [ ]
- [ ]
- [ ]
- [ ]
- [ ]
- [ ]
- [ ]
- [ ]
- [ ]
- [ ]
- [ ]
- [ ]
- [ ]
- [ ]

APPOINTMENTS & MEETINGS

DATE	TIME	VENDOR	PURPOSE

Weekly Wedding Planning

WEEK OF: _____

MONDAY

TUESDAY

WEDNESDAY

THURSDAY

FRIDAY

SATURDAY

WEDDING TO DO LIST

- [ ] _____
- [ ] _____
- [ ] _____
- [ ] _____
- [ ] _____
- [ ] _____
- [ ] _____
- [ ] _____
- [ ] _____
- [ ] _____
- [ ] _____
- [ ] _____
- [ ] _____
- [ ] _____
- [ ] _____
- [ ] _____
- [ ] _____

APPOINTMENTS & MEETINGS

DATE	TIME	VENDOR	PURPOSE

Weekly Wedding Planning

WEEK OF: _____

MONDAY

TUESDAY

WEDNESDAY

THURSDAY

FRIDAY

SATURDAY

WEDDING TO DO LIST

☐
☐
☐
☐
☐
☐
☐
☐
☐
☐
☐
☐
☐
☐
☐
☐
☐
☐

APPOINTMENTS & MEETINGS

DATE	TIME	VENDOR	PURPOSE

Weekly Wedding Planning

WEEK OF: _____

MONDAY

TUESDAY

WEDNESDAY

THURSDAY

FRIDAY

SATURDAY

WEDDING TO DO LIST

- [ ] _____
- [ ] _____
- [ ] _____
- [ ] _____
- [ ] _____
- [ ] _____
- [ ] _____
- [ ] _____
- [ ] _____
- [ ] _____
- [ ] _____
- [ ] _____
- [ ] _____
- [ ] _____
- [ ] _____
- [ ] _____
- [ ] _____

APPOINTMENTS & MEETINGS

DATE	TIME	VENDOR	PURPOSE

Weekly Wedding Planning

WEEK OF: _____

MONDAY

TUESDAY

WEDNESDAY

THURSDAY

FRIDAY

SATURDAY

WEDDING TO DO LIST

☐ _____
☐ _____
☐ _____
☐ _____
☐ _____
☐ _____
☐ _____
☐ _____
☐ _____
☐ _____
☐ _____
☐ _____
☐ _____
☐ _____
☐ _____
☐ _____
☐ _____
☐ _____

APPOINTMENTS & MEETINGS

DATE	TIME	VENDOR	PURPOSE

Weekly Wedding Planning

WEEK OF: _____

MONDAY

TUESDAY

WEDNESDAY

THURSDAY

FRIDAY

SATURDAY

WEDDING TO DO LIST

- [ ]
- [ ]
- [ ]
- [ ]
- [ ]
- [ ]
- [ ]
- [ ]
- [ ]
- [ ]
- [ ]
- [ ]
- [ ]
- [ ]
- [ ]
- [ ]
- [ ]
- [ ]

APPOINTMENTS & MEETINGS

DATE	TIME	VENDOR	PURPOSE

Weekly Wedding Planning

WEEK OF: _____

MONDAY

TUESDAY

WEDNESDAY

THURSDAY

FRIDAY

SATURDAY

WEDDING TO DO LIST

- [ ]
- [ ]
- [ ]
- [ ]
- [ ]
- [ ]
- [ ]
- [ ]
- [ ]
- [ ]
- [ ]
- [ ]
- [ ]
- [ ]
- [ ]
- [ ]
- [ ]

APPOINTMENTS & MEETINGS

DATE	TIME	VENDOR	PURPOSE

Weekly Wedding Planning

WEEK OF: _____

MONDAY

TUESDAY

WEDNESDAY

THURSDAY

FRIDAY

SATURDAY

WEDDING TO DO LIST

- [ ] _____
- [ ] _____
- [ ] _____
- [ ] _____
- [ ] _____
- [ ] _____
- [ ] _____
- [ ] _____
- [ ] _____
- [ ] _____
- [ ] _____
- [ ] _____
- [ ] _____
- [ ] _____
- [ ] _____
- [ ] _____
- [ ] _____
- [ ] _____

APPOINTMENTS & MEETINGS

DATE	TIME	VENDOR	PURPOSE

Weekly Wedding Planning

WEEK OF: _____

MONDAY

TUESDAY

WEDNESDAY

THURSDAY

FRIDAY

SATURDAY

WEDDING TO DO LIST

APPOINTMENTS & MEETINGS

DATE	TIME	VENDOR	PURPOSE

Weekly Wedding Planning

WEEK OF: _____

MONDAY

TUESDAY

WEDNESDAY

THURSDAY

FRIDAY

SATURDAY

WEDDING TO DO LIST

- ☐ _____
- ☐ _____
- ☐ _____
- ☐ _____
- ☐ _____
- ☐ _____
- ☐ _____
- ☐ _____
- ☐ _____
- ☐ _____
- ☐ _____
- ☐ _____
- ☐ _____
- ☐ _____
- ☐ _____
- ☐ _____
- ☐ _____

APPOINTMENTS & MEETINGS

DATE	TIME	VENDOR	PURPOSE

Weekly Wedding Planning

WEEK OF:

MONDAY

TUESDAY

WEDNESDAY

THURSDAY

FRIDAY

SATURDAY

WEDDING TO DO LIST

APPOINTMENTS & MEETINGS

DATE	TIME	VENDOR	PURPOSE

Weekly Wedding Planning

WEEK OF: _____

MONDAY	WEDDING TO DO LIST

MONDAY

TUESDAY

WEDNESDAY

THURSDAY

FRIDAY

SATURDAY

WEDDING TO DO LIST

☐ _____
☐ _____
☐ _____
☐ _____
☐ _____
☐ _____
☐ _____
☐ _____
☐ _____
☐ _____
☐ _____
☐ _____
☐ _____
☐ _____
☐ _____
☐ _____
☐ _____
☐ _____

APPOINTMENTS & MEETINGS

DATE	TIME	VENDOR	PURPOSE

Weekly Wedding Planning

WEEK OF: _____

MONDAY

TUESDAY

WEDNESDAY

THURSDAY

FRIDAY

SATURDAY

WEDDING TO DO LIST

- [ ] _____
- [ ] _____
- [ ] _____
- [ ] _____
- [ ] _____
- [ ] _____
- [ ] _____
- [ ] _____
- [ ] _____
- [ ] _____
- [ ] _____
- [ ] _____
- [ ] _____
- [ ] _____
- [ ] _____
- [ ] _____
- [ ] _____
- [ ] _____

APPOINTMENTS & MEETINGS

DATE	TIME	VENDOR	PURPOSE

Weekly Wedding Planning

WEEK OF: _____

MONDAY

TUESDAY

WEDNESDAY

THURSDAY

FRIDAY

SATURDAY

WEDDING TO DO LIST

☐ _____
☐ _____
☐ _____
☐ _____
☐ _____
☐ _____
☐ _____
☐ _____
☐ _____
☐ _____
☐ _____
☐ _____
☐ _____
☐ _____
☐ _____
☐ _____

APPOINTMENTS & MEETINGS

DATE	TIME	VENDOR	PURPOSE

Wedding Planner
- PLANNING GUIDELINE -

12 months BEFORE WEDDING

- SET THE DATE
- SET YOUR BUDGET
- CONSIDER WEDDING THEMES
- PLAN ENGAGEMENT PARTY
- RESEARCH POSSIBLE VENUES
- START RESEARCHING GOWNS
- RESEARCH PHOTOGRAPHERS
- RESEARCH VIDEOGRAPHERS
- RESEARCH DJS/ENTERTAINMENT

- CONSIDER FLORISTS
- RESEARCH CATERERS
- DECIDE ON OFFICIANT
- CREATE INITIAL GUEST LIST
- CHOOSE WEDDING PARTY
- CONSIDER ACCESSORIES
- REGISTER WITH GIFT REGISTRY
- DISCUSS HONEYMOON IDEAS
- RESEARCH WEDDING RINGS

- CONSIDER MUSIC CHOICES
- DECIDE ON OFFICIANT
- CONSIDER TRANSPORTATION
- CREATE INITIAL GUEST LIST
- CHOOSE WEDDING PARTY
- BRIDEMAIDS GOWNS
- BOOK TENTATIVE HOTELS
- CONSIDER BEAUTY SALONS
- CONSIDER SHOES & OTHER

Things To Do	Status

TOP PRIORITIES

NOTES & IDEAS

APPOINTMENTS & REMINDERS

Wedding Planner

- PLANNING GUIDELINE -

9 Months BEFORE WEDDING

- [ ] FINALIZE GUEST LIST
- [ ] ORDER INVITATIONS
- [ ] PLAN YOUR RECEPTION
- [ ] BOOK PHOTOGRAPHER
- [ ] BOOK VIDEOGRAPHER
- [ ] CHOOSE WEDDING GOWN
- [ ] ORDER BRIDESMAIDS DRESSES
- [ ] RESERVE TUXEDOS
- [ ] ARRANGE TRANSPORTATION
- [ ] BOOK WEDDING VENUE
- [ ] BOOK RECEPTION VENUE
- [ ] PLAN HONEYMOON
- [ ] BOOK FLORIST
- [ ] BOOK DJ/ENTERTAINMENT
- [ ] BOOK CATERER
- [ ] CHOOSE WEDDING CAKE
- [ ] BOOK OFFICIANT
- [ ] BOOK ROOMS FOR GUESTS

Things To Do	Status

TOP PRIORITIES

NOTES & IDEAS

APPOINTMENTS & REMINDERS

Wedding Planner

- PLANNING GUIDELINE -

6 months BEFORE WEDDING

- ORDER THANK YOU NOTES
- REVIEW RECEPTION DETAILS
- MAKE APPT FOR FITTING
- CONFIRM BRIDAL DRESSES
- OBTAIN MARRIAGE LICENSE
- BOOK HAIR STYLIST

- BOOK NAIL SALON
- CONFIRM MUSIC SELECTION
- WRITE VOWS
- PLAN BRIDAL SHOWER
- PLAN REHEARSAL
- BOOK REHEARSAL DINNER

- SHOP FOR WEDDING RINGS
- PLAN DECORATIONS
- CHOOSE BOUQUET TYPE
- FINALIZE GUEST LIST
- UPDATE PASSPORTS
- CONFIRM HOTEL ROOMS

Things To Do | Status

TOP PRIORITIES

NOTES & IDEAS

APPOINTMENTS & REMINDERS

Wedding Planner

4 Months BEFORE WEDDING

- PLANNING GUIDELINE -

- [ ] MAIL OUT INVITATIONS
- [ ] MEET WITH OFFICIANT
- [ ] BUY WEDDING FAVORS
- [ ] BUY WEDDING PARTY GIFTS
- [ ] PURCHASE SHOES
- [ ] FINALIZE THANK YOU CARDS

- [ ] FINALIZE HONEYMOON PLANS
- [ ] ATTEND FIRST DRESS FITTING
- [ ] FINALIZE VOWS
- [ ] FINALIZE RECEPTION MENU
- [ ] KEEP TRACK OF RSVPS
- [ ] BOOK PHOTO SESSION

- [ ] CONFIRM CATERER
- [ ] FINALIZE RING FITTING
- [ ] CONFIRM FLOWERS
- [ ] CONFIRM BAND
- [ ] SHOP FOR HONEYMOON
- [ ] BUY GARTER BELT

Things To Do	Status

TOP PRIORITIES

NOTES & IDEAS

APPOINTMENTS & REMINDERS

Wedding Planner
- PLANNING GUIDELINE -

1 month BEFORE WEDDING

- CHOOSE YOUR MC
- REQUEST SPECIAL TOASTS
- ARRANGE TRANSPORTATION
- CHOOSE YOUR HAIR STYLE
- CHOOSE YOUR NAIL COLOR
- ATTEND BRIDAL SHOWER

- CONFIRM CAKE CHOICES
- CONFIRM MENU (FINAL)
- CONFIRM SEATING
- CONFIRM VIDEOGRAPHER
- ARRANGE LEGAL DOCS
- FINALIZE WEDDING DUTIES

- CONFIRM BRIDESMAID DRESSES
- MEET WITH DJ/MC
- FINAL DRESS FITTING
- WRAP WEDDIING PARTY GIFTS
- CONFIRM FINAL GUEST COUNT
- CREATE WEDDING SCHEDULE

Things To Do | Status

TOP PRIORITIES

NOTES & IDEAS

APPOINTMENTS & REMINDERS

Wedding Planner
- PLANNING GUIDELINE -

1 Week BEFORE WEDDING

- [ ] PAYMENT TO VENDORS
- [ ] PACK FOR HONEYMOON
- [ ] CONFIRM HOTEL RESERVATION
- [ ] GIVE SCHEDULE TO PARTY
- [ ] DELIVER LICENSE TO OFFICIANT
- [ ] CONFIRM WITH VENDORS

- [ ] PICK UP WEDDING DRESS
- [ ] PICK UP TUXEDOS
- [ ] GIVE MUSIC LIST TO DJ/BAND
- [ ] CONFIRM SHOES/HEELS FIT
- [ ] CONFIRM TRANSPORTATION
- [ ] MONEY FOR GRATUITIES

- [ ] COMPLETE MAKE UP TRIAL
- [ ] CONFIRM RINGS FIT
- [ ] CONFIRM TRAVEL PLANS
- [ ] CONFIRM HOTELS FOR GUESTS
- [ ] OTHER: _____
- [ ] OTHER: _____

Things To Do	Status

TOP PRIORITIES

NOTES & IDEAS

APPOINTMENTS & REMINDERS

Wedding Planner
- PLANNING GUIDELINE -

1 Day BEFORE WEDDING

- ATTEND REHEARSAL DINNER
- FINISH HONEYMOON PACKING
- GREET OUT OF TOWN GUESTS
- GET MANICURE/PEDICURE
- CHECK ON WEDDING VENUE
- CHECK WEATHER TO PREPARE
- GIVE GIFTS TO WEDDING PARTY
- CONFIRM RINGS FIT
- GET A GOOD NIGHT'S SLEEP

Things To Do	Status

TOP PRIORITIES

NOTES & IDEAS

APPOINTMENTS & REMINDERS

Your Special Day!

Day of WEDDING

- GET YOUR HAIR DONE
- GET YOUR MAKE UP DONE
- HAVE A LIGHT BREAKFAST
- MEET WITH BRIDAL PARTY
- GIVE RINGS TO BEST MAN
- ENJOY YOUR SPECIAL DAY!

Wedding Attire Planner

WEDDING ATTIRE EXPENSE TRACKER			
ITEM/PURCHASE	STATUS ✓	DATE PAID	TOTAL COST

NOTES & REMINDERS

TOTAL COST:

Notes:

WEDDING ATTIRE DETAILS

Venue Planner

VENUE EXPENSE TRACKER

ITEM/PURCHASE	STATUS ✓	DATE PAID	TOTAL COST

NOTES & REMINDERS

TOTAL COST:

Notes:

VENUE PLANNING DETAILS

Catering Planner

CATERING EXPENSE TRACKER			
ITEM/PURCHASE	STATUS ✓	DATE PAID	TOTAL COST

NOTES & REMINDERS

TOTAL COST:

Notes:

CATERING PLANNER DETAILS

Entertainment Planner

ENTERTAINMENT EXPENSE TRACKER

ITEM/PURCHASE	STATUS ✓	DATE PAID	TOTAL COST

NOTES & REMINDERS

TOTAL COST:

Notes:

Love

ENTERTAINMENT DETAILS

Videographer Planner

Videographer Expense Tracker

ITEM/PURCHASE	STATUS ✓	DATE PAID	TOTAL COST

NOTES & REMINDERS

TOTAL COST:

Notes:

Videographer Details

Photographer Planner

PHOTOGRAPHER EXPENSE TRACKER			
ITEM/PURCHASE	STATUS ✓	DATE PAID	TOTAL COST

NOTES & REMINDERS

TOTAL COST:

Notes:

PHOTOGRAPHER DETAILS

Florist Planner

FLORIST EXPENSE TRACKER

ITEM/PURCHASE	STATUS ✓	DATE PAID	TOTAL COST

NOTES & REMINDERS

TOTAL COST:

Notes:

FLORIST PLANNING DETAILS

Extra Wedding Costs

ITEM/PURCHASE	STATUS ✓	DATE PAID	TOTAL COST

MISC WEDDING EXPENSE TRACKER

NOTES & REMINDERS

TOTAL COST:

Notes:

MISC WEDDING DETAILS

Bachelorette Party Planner

EVENT DETAILS

DATE

TIME

VENUE

THEME

HOST

OTHER

SCHEDULE OF EVENTS

TIME	

GUEST LIST

FIRST NAME	LAST NAME	R

SUPPLIES & SHOPPING LIST

- [ ]
- [ ]
- [ ]
- [ ]
- [ ]
- [ ]
- [ ]
- [ ]
- [ ]
- [ ]
- [ ]
- [ ]
- [ ]
- [ ]
- [ ]
- [ ]
- [ ]
- [ ]

NOTES & REMINDERS

love

Bachelor Party Planner

EVENT DETAILS

DATE

TIME

VENUE

THEME

HOST

OTHER

SCHEDULE OF EVENTS

TIME	

GUEST LIST

FIRST NAME	LAST NAME	R

SUPPLIES & SHOPPING LIST

- [ ]
- [ ]
- [ ]
- [ ]
- [ ]
- [ ]
- [ ]
- [ ]
- [ ]
- [ ]
- [ ]
- [ ]
- [ ]
- [ ]
- [ ]
- [ ]
- [ ]

NOTES & REMINDERS

love

Reception Planner

MEAL PLANNER IDEAS

HORS D'OEUVRES

1st COURSE:

2nd COURSE:

3rd COURSE:

4th COURSE:

MEAL PLANNING NOTES

Wedding Planning Notes

IDEAS & REMINDERS

Wedding to do List

PLANNING FOR THE BIG DAY

Wedding Guest List

NAME	ADDRESS	PHONE #	# IN PARTY	RSVP: ✓

Wedding Guest List

NAME	ADDRESS	PHONE #	# IN PARTY	RSVP: ✓

Wedding Guest List

NAME	ADDRESS	PHONE #	# IN PARTY	RSVP: ✓

Wedding Guest List

NAME	ADDRESS	PHONE #	# IN PARTY	RSVP: ✓

Wedding Guest List

NAME	ADDRESS	PHONE #	# IN PARTY	RSVP: ✓

Wedding Guest List

NAME	ADDRESS	PHONE #	# IN PARTY	RSVP: ✓

Wedding Guest List

NAME	ADDRESS	PHONE #	# IN PARTY	RSVP: ✓

Wedding Guest List

NAME	ADDRESS	PHONE #	# IN PARTY	RSVP: ✓

Wedding Guest List

NAME	ADDRESS	PHONE #	# IN PARTY	RSVP: ✓

Wedding Guest List

NAME	ADDRESS	PHONE #	# IN PARTY	RSVP: ✓

Wedding Seating Chart

Table #

TABLE #:
1:
2:
3:
4:
5:
6:
7:
8:

love

Table #

TABLE #:
1:
2:
3:
4:
5:
6:
7:
8:

Wedding Seating Chart

Table #

TABLE #:
1 :
2 :
3 :
4 :
5 :
6 :
7 :
8 :

love

Table #

TABLE #:
1 :
2 :
3 :
4 :
5 :
6 :
7 :
8 :

Wedding Seating Chart

Table #

TABLE #:

1:

2:

3:

4:

5:

6:

7:

8:

Table #

TABLE #:

1:

2:

3:

4:

5:

6:

7:

8:

Wedding Seating Chart

Table #

Table #

TABLE #:

1:

2:

3:

4:

5:

6:

7:

8:

TABLE #:

1:

2:

3:

4:

5:

6:

7:

8:

Wedding Seating Chart

Table #

TABLE #:

1:

2:

3:

4:

5:

6:

7:

8:

Table #

TABLE #:

1:

2:

3:

4:

5:

6:

7:

8:

Wedding Seating Chart

Table #

TABLE #:

1:

2:

3:

4:

5:

6:

7:

8:

Table #

TABLE #:

1:

2:

3:

4:

5:

6:

7:

8:

Wedding Seating Chart

Table #

Table #

TABLE #:

1:

2:

3:

4:

5:

6:

7:

8:

TABLE #:

1:

2:

3:

4:

5:

6:

7:

8:

Wedding Seating Chart

Table #

TABLE #:

1:

2:

3:

4:

5:

6:

7:

8:

Table #

TABLE #:

1:

2:

3:

4:

5:

6:

7:

8:

Wedding Seating Chart

Table #

TABLE #:

1 :

2 :

3 :

4 :

5 :

6 :

7 :

8 :

Table #

TABLE #:

1 :

2 :

3 :

4 :

5 :

6 :

7 :

8 :

Wedding Seating Chart

Table #

Table #

TABLE #:

1:

2:

3:

4:

5:

6:

7:

8:

TABLE #:

1:

2:

3:

4:

5:

6:

7:

8:

Wedding Seating Chart

Table #

TABLE #:

1:

2:

3:

4:

5:

6:

7:

8:

Table #

TABLE #:

1:

2:

3:

4:

5:

6:

7:

8:

Wedding Seating Chart

Table #

TABLE #:
1:
2:
3:
4:
5:
6:
7:
8:

Table #

TABLE #:
1:
2:
3:
4:
5:
6:
7:
8:

Wedding Seating Chart

Table #

TABLE #:

1:

2:

3:

4:

5:

6:

7:

8:

Table #

TABLE #:

1:

2:

3:

4:

5:

6:

7:

8:

Wedding Seating Chart

Table #

TABLE #:

1:

2:

3:

4:

5:

6:

7:

8:

Table #

TABLE #:

1:

2:

3:

4:

5:

6:

7:

8:

Wedding Seating Chart

Table #

TABLE #:

1:

2:

3:

4:

5:

6:

7:

8:

Table #

TABLE #:

1:

2:

3:

4:

5:

6:

7:

8:

Wedding Seating Chart

Table #

TABLE #:

1:

2:

3:

4:

5:

6:

7:

8:

Table #

TABLE #:

1:

2:

3:

4:

5:

6:

7:

8:

Wedding Seating Chart

Table #

TABLE #:

1 :

2 :

3 :

4 :

5 :

6 :

7 :

8 :

Table #

TABLE #:

1 :

2 :

3 :

4 :

5 :

6 :

7 :

8 :

Wedding Seating Chart

TABLE #:

1:

2:

3:

4:

5:

6:

7:

8:

Table #

TABLE #:

1:

2:

3:

4:

5:

6:

7:

8:

Table #

Wedding Seating Chart

Table #

Table #

TABLE #:

1:

2:

3:

4:

5:

6:

7:

8:

TABLE #:

1:

2:

3:

4:

5:

6:

7:

8:

Wedding Seating Chart

TABLE #:

1:

2:

3:

4:

5:

6:

7:

8:

TABLE #:

1:

2:

3:

4:

5:

6:

7:

8:

Wedding Seating Chart

Table #

Table #

TABLE #:

1:

2:

3:

4:

5:

6:

7:

8:

TABLE #:

1:

2:

3:

4:

5:

6:

7:

8:

Wedding Seating Chart

Table #

TABLE #:

1:

2:

3:

4:

5:

6:

7:

8:

Table #

TABLE #:

1:

2:

3:

4:

5:

6:

7:

8:

Wedding Seating Chart

Table #

TABLE #:

1 :

2 :

3 :

4 :

5 :

6 :

7 :

8 :

Table #

TABLE #:

1 :

2 :

3 :

4 :

5 :

6 :

7 :

8 :

Wedding Seating Chart

Table #

TABLE #:

1:

2:

3:

4:

5:

6:

7:

8:

Table #

TABLE #:

1:

2:

3:

4:

5:

6:

7:

8:

Wedding Seating Chart

Table

TABLE #:

1:

2:

3:

4:

5:

6:

7:

8:

Table

TABLE #:

1:

2:

3:

4:

5:

6:

7:

8:

Wedding Seating Chart

Table #

TABLE #:

1:

2:

3:

4:

5:

6:

7:

8:

Table #

TABLE #:

1:

2:

3:

4:

5:

6:

7:

8:

Wedding Seating Chart

Table #

TABLE #:

| 1: | 2: | 3: | 4: | 5: | 6: | 7: | 8: |
| 9: | 10: | 11: | 12: | 13: | 14: | 15: | 16: |

Table #

TABLE #:

| 1: | 2: | 3: | 4: | 5: | 6: | 7: | 8: |
| 9: | 10: | 11: | 12: | 13: | 14: | 15: | 16: |

Wedding Seating Chart

Table #

TABLE #:

| 1: | 2: | 3: | 4: | 5: | 6: | 7: | 8: |
| 9: | 10: | 11: | 12: | 13: | 14: | 15: | 16: |

Table #

TABLE #:

| 1: | 2: | 3: | 4: | 5: | 6: | 7: | 8: |
| 9: | 10: | 11: | 12: | 13: | 14: | 15: | 16: |

Wedding Seating Chart

Table #

TABLE #:

| 1: | 2: | 3: | 4: | 5: | 6: | 7: | 8: |
| 9: | 10: | 11: | 12: | 13: | 14: | 15: | 16: |

Table #

TABLE #:

| 1: | 2: | 3: | 4: | 5: | 6: | 7: | 8: |
| 9: | 10: | 11: | 12: | 13: | 14: | 15: | 16: |

Wedding Seating Chart

Table #

TABLE #:

| 1: | 2: | 3: | 4: | 5: | 6: | 7: | 8: |
| 9: | 10: | 11: | 12: | 13: | 14: | 15: | 16: |

Table #

TABLE #:

| 1: | 2: | 3: | 4: | 5: | 6: | 7: | 8: |
| 9: | 10: | 11: | 12: | 13: | 14: | 15: | 16: |

Wedding Seating Chart

Table

TABLE #:

| 1: | 2: | 3: | 4: | 5: | 6: | 7: | 8: |
| 9: | 10: | 11: | 12: | 13: | 14: | 15: | 16: |

Table

TABLE #:

| 1: | 2: | 3: | 4: | 5: | 6: | 7: | 8: |
| 9: | 10: | 11: | 12: | 13: | 14: | 15: | 16: |

Wedding Seating Chart

Table #

TABLE #:
1:        2:   3:   4:   5:   6:   7:   8:
9:        10:   11:   12:   13:   14:   15:   16:

Table #

TABLE #:
1:        2:   3:   4:   5:   6:   7:   8:
9:        10:   11:   12:   13:   14:   15:   16:

Wedding Seating Chart

Table #

TABLE #:

| 1: | 2: | 3: | 4: | 5: | 6: | 7: | 8: |
| 9: | 10: | 11: | 12: | 13: | 14: | 15: | 16: |

Table #

TABLE #:

| 1: | 2: | 3: | 4: | 5: | 6: | 7: | 8: |
| 9: | 10: | 11: | 12: | 13: | 14: | 15: | 16: |

Wedding Seating Chart

Table #

TABLE #:

| 1: | 2: | 3: | 4: | 5: | 6: | 7: | 8: |
| 9: | 10: | 11: | 12: | 13: | 14: | 15: | 16: |

Table #

TABLE #:

| 1: | 2: | 3: | 4: | 5: | 6: | 7: | 8: |
| 9: | 10: | 11: | 12: | 13: | 14: | 15: | 16: |

Wedding Seating Chart

Table #

TABLE #:

| 1: | 2: | 3: | 4: | 5: | 6: | 7: | 8: |
| 9: | 10: | 11: | 12: | 13: | 14: | 15: | 16: |

Table #

TABLE #:

| 1: | 2: | 3: | 4: | 5: | 6: | 7: | 8: |
| 9: | 10: | 11: | 12: | 13: | 14: | 15: | 16: |

Wedding Seating Chart

Table

TABLE #:

| 1: | 2: | 3: | 4: | 5: | 6: | 7: | 8: |
| 9: | 10: | 11: | 12: | 13: | 14: | 15: | 16: |

Table

TABLE #:

| 1: | 2: | 3: | 4: | 5: | 6: | 7: | 8: |
| 9: | 10: | 11: | 12: | 13: | 14: | 15: | 16: |

Wedding Seating Chart

Table

TABLE #:

| 1: | 2: | 3: | 4: | 5: | 6: | 7: | 8: |
| 9: | 10: | 11: | 12: | 13: | 14: | 15: | 16: |

Table

TABLE #:

| 1: | 2: | 3: | 4: | 5: | 6: | 7: | 8: |
| 9: | 10: | 11: | 12: | 13: | 14: | 15: | 16: |

Wedding Planning Notes

IDEAS & REMINDERS

Wedding to do List
PLANNING FOR THE BIG DAY

Wedding Planning Notes

IDEAS & REMINDERS

Wedding to do List

PLANNING FOR THE BIG DAY

Wedding Planning Notes

IDEAS & REMINDERS

Wedding to do List
PLANNING FOR THE BIG DAY

Wedding Planning Notes

IDEAS & REMINDERS

Wedding to do List
PLANNING FOR THE BIG DAY

Wedding Planning Notes

IDEAS & REMINDERS

Wedding to do List
PLANNING FOR THE BIG DAY

Made in the USA
Columbia, SC
02 July 2023

19928576R00061